Little Pink Golf Book: by Abbey Gittings

Published by: Amazon/Abbey Gittings

abbeygittingsgolfcoaching.com

Copyright © 2022 Abbey Gittings

Cover by Abbey Gittings

ISBN: 9798778489073

Number 1 Edition

Little Pink Golf Book

Abbey Gittings

Hey girls, and welcome to my Little Pink Golf Book!

The reason for writing this book is because I want more women & girls to learn, love & continue to play the game of golf. I believe that with my years of teaching, playing and coaching experience, I can help bring you some insight into how to survive the crazy journey that is playing golf.... and boy is it crazy!
I hope to make you feel comfortable within the golfing world, give you tips and tricks to help you along the way, and bring a smile to your face.

I want to let you know that you are not alone in thinking that sometimes you aren't good enough to play on the course, or that you're never going to get consistent or good at the game because SO many ladies think the same. However, I want to change these thoughts and let each and every one of you to know that you are good enough, because YOU can do anything, and the golf world is lucky to have you in it!

I know sometimes being a woman in sport can feel like you already have the world against you, but I am here to help you smash through that fear, break through the barriers and enjoy the game that has bought me so much pleasure for so many years.

Love Abbey ♡

Chapter 1

About Me

So, let's start with a little introduction to who I am, and my golfing journey to date...

My name is Abbey Gittings, and I was born just outside Birmingham, England. I have played golf ever since I can remember, and I am now a fully qualified PGA Golf Professional coaching the game I love.

Golf is a huge part of my life, and always has been, and now my biggest focus is sharing my passion to help grow the women's game. This book was created in realisation that there isn't anything out there specifically for us golfing girls, which I felt needed to change. Now I don't have to tell you twice that we are wired very differently to men (in a much better way of course) which is why I felt it was my duty to bring you all a book written in our own "women's language".
You girls are my daily inspiration to keep doing what I am doing, and I want to help you on your golfing journey as much as possible.

But first, I wanted to tell you a little bit about my story and the path I have taken to get where I am today....

Early Life

So, my adventures in golf started when I was just 5 years old, and I was one of those kids that extremely high energy levels. I enjoyed playing any sport I possibly could, which meant that when my grandad came home from a car boot sale one afternoon with a set of kids' golf clubs and asked if I wanted to start taking golf lessons, I jumped at the chance.

(My grandad Clive)

My grandad arranged for me to take part in junior group lessons at The Belfry Golf Club, in a class that was only 45 minutes every Saturday morning. It was my favourite time of the week. After a couple of years of lessons, I was scouted by the Warwickshire County Ladies and soon was very proud to be playing for the county girls' team.

From that moment on golf became a very big part of my life....

My Amateur Career

As an amateur golfer I played in far too many events to count or write down (plus I don't want to bore you to sleep), but a few that stand out in my head would be the county championships, County match week, the English championships, the British championships, the Faldo Series & my collegiate golf in America.

I have so many incredible memories from those years, and I would love to share them all with you, but like I said there are far too many and I think I would need to write a whole other book to find the space haha. So, let's just go through a few...

Playing County golf will always be something so close to my heart because that is where it all really started for me. There was something so special about playing for your county and being part of a team, and I believe that it was the feeling of community I received from the Warwickshire County team that gave me the strength to keep pursuing the game. Us girls are stronger when we stick together!

I was also so lucky over the years to have the opportunity to play in multiple English & British championships at some amazing course all over the UK & Ireland. To this day I will never forget coming down the last hole at Carnoustie in the British Ladies, playing my shot towards the iconic clock on the hotel, or finally making my first cut in the event. The memories that I

7

have from these events though don't come from victories, or wins, but instead from the experiences I had when playing them. I think that is important, that I never valued myself or my golf on how well I did, but instead on how much fun I was having.

Another moment of happiness was when I made it through to the Grand Final of the Faldo Series, which was to be played at a course in Brazil. This was when I was 18 and it was the first time I had been abroad in my life, let alone played golf abroad! That being said, my biggest memory from that event was extreme heat, sweating a lot, and having no idea how I was going to make it walking around the 18 holes. It was an incredible experience though, and I am forever grateful to Nick Faldo for holding those events for junior golfers, which he still does now.

Now as I have just mentioned, I didn't really get on too well with the heat in Brazil. However, when I was offered a full scholarship to Nova Southeastern University in Ft Lauderdale, Florida, there was no way I was going to turn down sunshine, palm trees and incredible golf courses.

I started my first semester for the NSU women's golf team in August 2009 and graduated from there in May 2013. The 4 years that I spent over the pond were some of the best experiences I've ever had and memories that I will keep with me forever.
Those who know me well know that I love to talk endlessly about my time in America! I mean do you remember that girl in the American pie movie who was always saying "This one time, at band camp". Well, that is me but change that sentence to "this one time at College" ha. I still to this day am a very hardcore NSU Shark (A shark was our college mascot) and I am very proud to call myself an alumni of the college.

So anyway, my actual journey in America...

As I said I went to America in 2009 when I was just 19 years old. It was my first time living away from home and I felt every emotion a human could possibly feel. I was terrified, nervous, excited, you name it I felt it. My dad had flown over with me for my first week to settle me in and make sure I had everything I needed, and I will never forget the day he dropped me off at the dorms before

getting his flight home – Niagara Falls type waterworks comes to mind!
Over my 4 years there I got to visit some incredible places and play some incredible golf courses. Some of the States we were lucky enough to visit were Washington DC, California, Arizona, Vegas, Hawaii and many more. It really was the best time of my life!

For me as a golfer, American courses really suited my game and I managed to have a successful College career whilst I was out there. I also think it was down to the fact that I was practicing 12pm-6pm every day during the week and all day long on the weekend, plus getting out on the course as much as I possibly could. The one big thing that I took away from my years in America was that the golf swing is only one part of the game and getting out on the course and really learning how to play out there, was an even bigger part. You could have the best swing in the world, but it is no use if you can only use It on the driving range. You need to be able to "play" the game, and only then can you survive the battlefield that is a golf course.

As I mentioned, I had quite a successful college career winning 5 tournaments individually, with the main highlight being winning the individual honours of the NCAA Division II National Championships in 2012, in Louisville Kentucky.

This is something that when I first started college seemed like a crazy, unreachable goal. However, in my Junior year I did it, and all with a dodgy looking swing & bad back. Never, ever think that a goal you set is unattainable. We all have the capability to achieve anything that we set our mind to!
Over my 4 years there I was also lucky enough to be part of a 3-time National Championship winning team, and it really did feel, and still does feel, amazing to be part of such an iconic, record-breaking golf team.

Professional Career

So, after I graduated College in 2013, I moved back to England and took the plunge to turn professional at an LET Access event in England, after receiving an invite to play. Now let me tell you, my first tournament as a professional golfer did not go as I had imagined in my head ha! I was cruising through the first 7 holes at 1 under par, and that was then when disaster struck. I managed to shank two balls out of bounds on hole 8 and walked away with a score of 10. (Now you'll learn the word Shank and what it is, but you will also learn to never say it out loud, almost like Voldemort in Harry Potter.)

After that first event I then went on to play the next 3 years on the LET Access Tour travelling around Europe. This was an incredible experience and I feel so lucky that I had the chance to be able to do this.

Unfortunately, I never won an event, but I did get close with a top 5 finish in the Northern Spain event (this was where I had my career low 67, which is a round I'll never forget)

Now whilst were on the topic of Spain, let's move on to my next adventure…

In 2016, I made the move to Spain's Costa Del Sol to become a golf coach. It was then that I began my 3-year PGA training (this is an online university degree through the University of Birmingham) and got stuck straight into the coaching life. Now 5 years later I am still in Spain and enjoying every day that I get to help someone with their golf game.

Golf has been my life since I was 5 years old, and has brought me so many unbelievable experiences, amazing memories and to be completely honest provided me with an amazing, happy and busy life.

By reading this book I want you all to be able to truly discover just how special this wonderful game is, and how much it can add to your life, on and off the course. I want to share with you the enjoyment and the excitement that this magical game can bring.

So,
get yourself a cup of tea, get comfy, and I hope you
enjoy this little introduction into the magical world of
golf.

Chapter 2

Why play golf?

The game of golf has something for everyone, and there are so many different reasons to play. Like I mentioned earlier, I started playing after my grandad picked me up a set of golf clubs from a car boot sale, and then took me to have junior group lessons. I still hold the memories I have from those days when I was younger so close to my heart. After that I think my love of the game grew from the enjoyment that I got from playing golf with my family & friends and the challenge itself of playing. It is the combination of these two things that has kept me playing all these years. (I won't say how long, or I will give away my age) I just know that it is always going to be a great day when I am stood on that first tee.

Like I said though, there are so many different reasons for playing golf, so let me take you through a few of them.

Great for your mental wellbeing

Golf may be one of the most frustrating games on the planet, as well as being one of the greatest, but it is also a game that helps you to forget all your other worries in the world. Whether you are stood on the range, or out playing in the sunshine on the course, golf is a great way to clear your mind and settle your soul.

For me, golf is the ultimate escape. When I am playing or practicing, my thoughts and emotions are focused solely on playing the shots I want to play rather than anything else. It is one of the purest forms of living in the moment, and is a place that I really enjoy being, my inner sanctuary almost. One very famous golfer likened playing golf to "going to the movies." For example, when you go to the movies, you are in a dark room, focused on only the movie, and distracted from your cares, worries, and the real world. It is the same thing with golf, it's just you, the ball and the flag.

Golf really can be SO frustrating, and I promise you it will more than likely drive you insane, but I can tell you one thing for sure... When you are slicing your driver out of bounds and raging about it, you are 100% not thinking about any of your real-world life problems.

Great form of exercise

The funny thing that people say about golf is that it is "A good walk ruined". However, it really is a great walk! I mean I bet you didn't know that a golf course can range between 3-6 miles long! Now I don't know about you, but for me that is a decent hike! Being able to get out into the fresh air alone for a few hours is a great way of looking after your mind & body.

I mean okay, it is not high intensity like tennis or football, but it is still a game that has a positive effect on your health and body. Growing up I always heard "Why are you working out for golf!?" or "Golf is just for fat old men" and it honestly used to drive me insane. Firstly, we don't all just drive around in buggies and secondly golf uses so many different muscles in the body.

Also any game that you can keep playing until you are older is awesome, right!? Keeping moving as you do get older is so important as it keeps you going. I mean my grandad was 73 when he passed away unfortunately from a short battle with Cancer, but before that he was still playing golf 3 or 4 times a week and was the fittest man I knew. I am sure it was down to him walking a golf course every week for years that kept him such an active person.

Every level of player can play together & enjoy a game of golf.

Whatever age, whatever level, it does not matter when it comes to a game of golf and everyone and anyone can play together and have the best time. This is also the case when it comes to competitions or even playing with your friends due to "handicaps". Everyone is set on a level playing field and anyone can win. This for me is one of the greatest things about golf because you can play to your own ability, yet still be able to enjoy a round of golf with your friends. I mean if you think about a game of tennis, a beginner player and an elite player are never going to be able to have a match together because their skill levels are so far apart. It would be way too hard for the beginner, yet way too easy for the professional and probably very unenjoyable for both. However, because golf is so individual, and you only play your own game, both amateurs & professionals can enjoy a round together. Meaning you can play with whoever you want to!

<u>A great way to socialise.</u>

Now I think this is one of the BEST things about golf, the socialising! Golf is a great way to spend time with your friends, or a great place to make new ones. Through playing golf over the years, I have made friendships that will last a lifetime, and friends that live all over the world.
I mean we all know as ladies that there is nothing better than time spent with our besties having a good old giggle and a gossip. Now how about 4 hours of that on the golf course with your favourite girls, followed by some lunch in the clubhouse. I really think we have found something very near to a perfect day out!

Challenge yourself & build up your self-confidence

Golf is the perfect way to really boost belief in yourself, help you grow stronger, learn perseverance and patience, and all in all help you to acquire better life skills. The challenge that golf brings will help you to understand your own self better than anything else. If you can learn to survive 18 holes on a golf course, then you can face anything life may throw at you.

I have grown as a person over the years, and the life skills I have acquired I really feel have come from playing the game myself. For one I am more patient, which I think is down to missing so many teeny tiny infuriating putts along the way.

Chapter 3

What´s in a Set of

Golf Clubs

So, the rule is that within a golf bag you can carry a maximum of 14 clubs, however, there is no "right" selection of the clubs that you must have, and each person's bag will be an individual mix of your own preferences.

For example, I don't have a 4 iron in my set (because I cannot use the damn thing haha) but instead choose to have a hybrid. Don't worry we will go through each of the different clubs on the next page...

Now, if you are only just starting out in golf, I would say that you only really need half a set of clubs to begin with. I would recommend that you start with, a putter, a sand wedge, pitching wedge, 9 iron, 7 iron, a hybrid and/or a beginners' driver. (Also, don't go spending a massive amount of money on a set in the beginning)

However, before you choose which clubs you want in your golf bag, I want to make sure you know all about the different kinds you will find in a set.
So, let's check them out....

The Driver

The driver aka the big one or "The big dog" (I don't know why it's called this, but you may hear some golfers say "let the big dog eat" which means, hit your driver ha)

The main goal of the driver is to get the ball down the fairway as far as possible, and it is the club we are usually going to use for our first shot off the tee from par 4´s & Par 5´s (and maybe the odd long par 3).

We are always going to put the ball on a tee peg when we are using this club.

Fairway Woods

The fairway wood is found within the "woods" category alongside the driver, however, is it a smaller headed version with a little more loft.

It is called "a wood" because back in the early days of golf, the clubs were made from persimmon wood and the shafts were made from hickory. (Look up hickory clubs on google for some blast from the past photos.)

Typically, the fairway woods are used for the second shot on par-5s or long par-4s, hence the term fairway in the name. However, they can also be used as the first shot on short par-4s or long par-3s.

You can typically find 3,4,5 & 7 woods.

Hybrid / Rescue Wood

The hybrid, which can sometimes be called a rescue wood, is a club that is a mixture of a long iron and a fairway wood put together.

These clubs can again be used from the fairway; however, their special ability is that they are designed to help lift the ball up into the air and out of poor lies. For example, if you find yourself in the rough beside the fairway, a hybrid is a great way to hit out of it, whilst still maintaining some distance with the shot.

As I mentioned before, these clubs are also a great option to hit from the fairway, especially for those players who sometimes struggle with fairway woods or with hitting through the ball. You will find these days, that many golfers will supplement their longer irons such as the 5 or 4 iron, for a hybrid instead, again due to the ease of hitting them.

Irons

Irons are the clubs in your bag that have a smaller clubhead than your woods, and the heads are made of metal.

You are going to use these clubs for your approach shots into greens, and sometimes as your tee shots off par 3's.

The irons are numbered 1 through 9, but the average golf set will contain a 4iron through 9iron, because the 1, 2 and 3 irons are the most difficult to hit.

"If you are caught on a golf course during a storm and are afraid of lightning, hold up a 1-iron, because not even God can hit a 1-iron"

The irons will have higher degrees of loft on them than the woods, with the 9-iron having the most loft and the 1 iron having the least loft.

Highest Loft   Lowest Loft

9   8   7   6   5   4   3   2   1

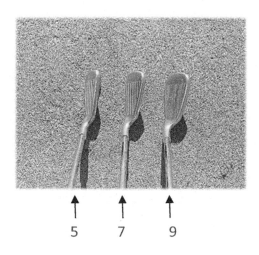

↑   ↑   ↑
5   7   9

More loft = Higher ball flight & less distance

Less loft = Lower ball flight & more distance

Wedges

Wedges are the highest-lofted clubs in the set and are used for the following golf shots:

- short approach shots (50 yards and in)
- strokes played out of the bunker
- chip shots
- pitch shots

The wedges can also be classified as "irons", but in my opinion are within their own little family of clubs.

Now the confusing part about wedges is there are so many different types that can be in a golfer's bag. In the old days it used to just be a "sandwedge" and a "pitching wedge", but in recent years & with more golf advancements there are now many more options which we will explore.

Pitching wedge (PW)

These are the lowest lofted of the wedges (the one that hits the ball the furthest) and are one of the basic clubs that every golfer carries.

Sand wedge (SW)

These were originally designed for hitting shots out of bunkers; however, they are now also used as a club for pitching also.

Gap wedge

Named a "gap" wedge because it fills in the loft gap between the PW and SW. This club has more loft than a PW, but less loft than a SW.

Lob wedge

This is normally the highest lofted club a golfer will carry and creates shots that will get up into the air very quickly. For example, shots that you want to hit onto the green with minimum roll (over a bunker to a close pin), or in some cases over a tree.

You may also notice some people have numbered wedges in their bag, such as a 54,58 or 60. This number relates to the amount of loft the club carries.

Putter

Your putter is the club you are going to use once you get onto the final part of the hole, which is the putting green. This club is one that comes in all different shapes & sizes; however, the one similarity is that they will all have a flat face.

This is the club you want to become best friends with, because as the well-known golf saying goes...

"Drive for show, putt for dough".

Chapter 4

The Different Golf Shots, what they are & how to play them

Putting

This is the shot we are playing when we are on the putting green (the end of the hole where the flag is) and where we are going to use the putter.

How to play it....

The Putting Stroke

- Ball position left of centre (helps us to hit up on the putt to give a lovely roll)
- Keep wrists quiet & firm
- Pendulum motion - With this stroke we are solely using our shoulders to rock backwards & forwards and your lower body will remain still.

- Eyes directly over the ball (you should be able to drop a ball from your eyes & land it on the ball below)

People generally believe that putting is the easiest part of the golf game. However, there is a lot more to putting than just the stroke itself, which makes putting one of the most complex of all the golf shots. So, let's see what else there is;

Aim

In simple terms this is pointing the clubface in the direction you want the ball to go. However, nothing in golf is simple haha! A great way to aim your ball, and in turn your clubface, is using the line already printed on your ball.

When you have picked where you want to aim, stand behind the ball, and point the line on your ball to this spot. You can then use the line on your putter to match the line on your ball and create the perfect visual aim to start the ball on your target.

Distance Control

This is commonly referred to as putting pace and controls the distance your putts go. If you can control your speed more effectively on the greens, you will get the ball closer to the hole. This means less putts and better scores!

Aim & distance control go hand in hand, and you need to get both correct if you are going to hole a putt. Too many times I have spent a long time getting the aim of a putt to then leave the ball short of the hole, it's so infuriating, but happens a lot! (it's all part of the fun I guess)

Putting unlike other shots in golf, really takes a lot of feel, and I believe that a high % of your golf practice should be on the putting green because of that.

<u>Reading the green</u>

Another part to putting that is massively essential to holing putts is "reading the green". This is exactly what it says on the tin and it is when we read the lay of the land using our eyes and senses, to figure out which way the ball will roll so we can determine our starting point. When we examine the grass between the ball and the hole, we need to determine the speed the putt will be (uphill/downhill) and any slopes that will alter the direction of the ball as it heads towards the hole.

"If you were to throw a bucket of water down the line of your putt, which way would the water run".

As I said putting is one part of the game that everyone thinks looks the easiest, however as you can see, there are so many different components to this shot that you need to learn and manage if you want putting success. This is why it is SO important for you to spend lots of your practice time working on your putting.

Golf Swing Set up

Body aim & club alignment

The first thing to keep in mind is that aim and alignment go together like tea & biscuits. We first aim the clubface to our target, and then we align our body (feet, hips & shoulders) at 90 degrees to the clubface to hit a straight shot.

One thing I do that has always helped me to aim the club face, comes as part of my pre shot routine (we will discuss what this is a little later). So, when I stand behind the ball to choose my target, I pick something on the ground in front of the ball, and try to line my club up with that, followed by my body. I find this much easier than trying to line up to a target in the distance.

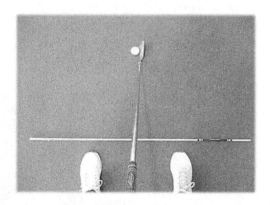

Grip

Okay, so how do we hold the club...
The grip is a fundamental part of the swing, as it leads the way for how we are going to swing the club.

We are going to start by placing your left hand on the club first, with the club running from the middle joint of your index finger to the base of your little finger. Gently then hold the club (try not to wrap your hands around the club), and we should see two and a half knuckles on show from front view.
You are then going to do the same with your right hand, just slightly lower than your left, so that your right hand will be covering your left thumb.
You will notice how in the completed golf grip the hands sit closely together, as if they are one unit. This is what we want to achieve so that the hands are working together, rather than fighting against one another.

When it comes to how hard we grip the club, you want to imagine that you are holding a baby bird. Tight enough that the bird cannot fly away, but not so tight that you crush it.

There are 3 different grip types when it comes to holding the club. The most used would be the interlock as this one really keeps the hands connected, and moving as one. However, go with whichever grip feels more natural and comfortable for you.

Interlock

Baseball

Overlap

Posture

Having the correct posture at address is an important fundamental, that is normally overlooked. Your posture helps to dictate how the club swings around your body, helps the body turn correctly, promotes good balance & also helps to protect you from any type of back injury.

When addressing the ball, check you are doing the following points to achieve the perfect posture;

- Tilt the top part of your body forwards from your hips
- Knees slightly bent (weight in balls of feet)
- Let your arms hang down in a relaxed rested position.
- Stance width depends on which club you are hitting

Boobs

"So, do I put my arms over my boobs, do I go under them, or do I just go around them".

This is a part of the golf game that men do not have to deal with (well, some men might haha), but it is a part that has a huge impact on a lady golfers swing. Honestly, this is one question that I have been asked so many times throughout the years from women, because no one really talks about it, and my response to this question is as follows;

100% NEVER go over the top as this leads to your arms locking out and tensing, which makes it tough to be able to make a full swing. Going under is also not beneficial to making a good golf swing, which kind of only really leaves us the option of "going around them".

There is a training aid in the golf world that a lot of professional's use called the smart ball, which you hold between your arms to help keep connection through your swing. Well, us ladies are lucky enough to have our very own in-built version haha!

This may sound hilariously outrageous, but honestly the most productive way to deal with your boobs, is to in fact use them. Use them to help keep your body and arms connected as one.

Chipping

A chip shot is a short, low shot that stays close to the ground, and spends more time on the floor than in the air (runs more). It is normally used around the side of the green, and when there are no obstacles to hit over between the ball and the hole.

How to play it..

- Narrow stance & ball position right of centre towards back foot
- Weight over left side (70%)
- Grip lower down on the grip for more control
- Using only our shoulders to rotate back & forwards (similar to a putting action). We want to make sure that our wrists are not going to flick on the follow through of the swing.

Set up

The swing

Pitching

A pitch shot is shorter, higher shot that spends more time in the air, than on the ground. It is normally used when there is an obstacle to hit over, such as a bunker or grass, between the ball and the hole. The distance for the shot is usually between 20-80 yards away.

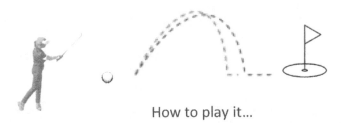

How to play it...

- Narrow stance & ball position right of centre towards back foot.
- Weight over left side (60%)
- Grip lower down on the grip for more control.
- Hinge the wrists in the backswing (L shape) but keep them firm through impact.
- Keep the weight over the left side throughout the swing & turn hips to face the target to finish.

Set up

40

The swing

Bunker Shots

A bunker shot is quite different compared to other shortgame shots, and one that is played out of the sand. (Unfortunately, they are not as fun as being at the beach)

The first thing to understand when playing this shot is that you are not actually contacting the ball, but in fact hitting the sand behind it. Your club is sliding underneath the ball, through the sand, by using the *bounce on your wedge. It is going to be the sand that is lifting your ball out of the bunker, rather than your golf club.

(*bounce is the angle formed between the leading edge of your clubface and the bottom of the club.)

As crazy as it sounds, the bunker shot is one of my favourites in golf, because I feel like it is the one shot you can really give your all too and be aggressive with. So, if you are ever in a bunker think of something that really annoyed you and use that as fire power.

How to play it

- The first thing you are going to do before anything is open your clubface and then grip the club. Too many people grip the club first and then open the clubface which leads to the hands rolling back to neutral at impact, and we lose the open clubface. So lay the clubface open, and then place your hands on the grip.
- Weight over left side (70%)
- Grip lower down on the grip for more control
- Strong wrists! We want to keep the clubface open which means "holding off our wrists" and not allowing a normal release.
- Aim your feet a little left of target due to opened clubface. (How much left will come with more practice & experience)

Set up

The swing

Iron Shots

As mentioned earlier, these are the shots we are likely to play for our approach shots into the green, using a club between our 9 and 4 iron.

<u>How to play it</u>

- Stance shoulder width apart
- Ball position changes with every club. 9 iron is placed in the middle of the stance, and as we go up the clubs, 8, 7, 6, 5, 4 we move the ball a little more towards the left foot.
- Hit down onto the ball with a downward strike.
- From top of the backswing transition your weight over to your left side and turn hips.

<u>Set up</u>

The Swing

Rescue/ Hybrid Club Shot

As mentioned before the hybrid or rescue clubs are a combination of long irons and fairway woods, which can be used off the fairway or to get out of the rough.

How to play it

- Stance shoulder width apart
- The ball should be placed forward of centre in the stance, a few inches inside the left heel.
- You should meet the ball with a downward strike, just like we do with an iron shot.

*(Swing sequence same as iron)

Set up

Fairway Woods

A fairway wood is the longest club that we can hit from the ground.

How to play it

- Stance a little wider than shoulder width
- The ball should be placed forward of centre in the stance, a few inches inside the left heel.
- You should meet the ball with a downward strike, again just like we do with an iron shot.
- From top of backswing transition your weight over to your left side and turn hips.

*(Swing sequence same as iron)

Set up

*Also, with any type of the above golf shots, whether that be a wedge shot, 6 iron, or hybrid, never try to "lift" the ball up yourself. Hitting down onto the ball & the natural loft on the club will do that for you.

A top tip I have for making sure you hit more down onto the ball is when you are practicing place a tee a couple of inches Infront of the ball (left of the ball). The aim is going to be to try and hit the tee after you have struck the ball.

Driving

This is the longest club in the bag which can also make it the hardest to control. (Do not let that put you off though, it can also be the most fun, and there is nothing better than hitting a bomb tee shot with a Driver) However, never get yourself down if this guy doesn't work for you some days, because we are all in the same boat ha!

How to play it

- Stance a little wider than shoulder width
- Ball placed forward in the stance towards the left foot. (I like to stand with my feet together in line with the ball, then, do a little step with my left foot & a big step with my right foot)
- Try to feel a lovely wide swing
- From top of backswing transition your weight over to your left side and turn hips
- Sweep the ball off the tee

Set up

The Swing

Sloping Lies

Uphill lie

When playing a shot from an uphill lie, you want to make sure you take more club. This is because the upward angle of the hill adds loft to the clubface.

Play the ball slightly more forward in your stance than normal (towards the left foot) and try to get your shoulders parallel to the hill (lean with the slope). With the swing, try to feel like you are swinging up the slope.

Shots from an uphill will tend to go left of the target, so make sure you aim your club and body a little right of the target to compensate.

Downhill lie

When playing a shot from a downhill lie, you want to make sure you take less club. This is because the hill delofts the club.

Position the ball back in your stance (towards the right foot) and try to get your shoulders parallel to the hill (lean with the slope). With the swing, try to resist the urge to lean back, but instead follow your swing down the slope.

Shots from a downhill lie will tend to go right of the target, so make sure you aim your club and body a little left of the target to compensate.

Ball below feet

When playing a shot from below your feet, the first thing you want to do is place your hands right at the top of your grip. This is because the ball is lower than our feet, making it further away from our body, meaning we need to use the whole length of our club so not to miss the ball completely.

You also want to make sure you get into a more squatted position at set up, with your weight on your heels to avoid falling forwards.

Because of this awkward squat position, body turn during the swing is restricted, and we cannot get through the ball. This can lead to the ball starting off to the right, so make sure you aim a little left at set up with your club & body.

Ball above feet

When playing a shot above your feet, the first thing you want to do is place your hands towards the bottom of your grip. This is because the ball is higher than our feet, making it closer to our body, meaning we need to use less length of our club to avoid hitting the ground early.

You also want to make sure you stand a little taller with this shot, with your weight more into your toes to fight against falling backwards.

From this upright posture, the swing will be flatter or more around the body, which creates more hand and arm rotation through the shot. This can lead to the ball starting off to the left, so make sure you aim a little right at set up with your club & body.

Chapter 5

Getting Started

So, you want to learn to play golf... but where do you start!?

My first piece of advice would be to take lessons. One of the great things about taking lessons early is that you haven't already ingrained any bad habits, which means you have a blank canvas to build your beautiful swing on. Your friends and partners might sometimes have good tips for you, but personally I would say that it is better to see a professional coach first, since they're the ones trained to teach, and will set you on the right path.

Also, I would say even when you feel competent enough to play on the course, it is always a good idea to continue with your lessons. That way you are always improving or maintaining rather than allowing faults to creep back into your game. Plus, from the range to the golf course is a completely different ball game, so it is always a great idea for a coach to be able to get out on the course with you to continue your development.

(Also, all professional golfers still see their coaches regularly, as unfortunately in golf, you will never maintain perfection. Such a frustrating, but truthful statement)

However, if you do wish to learn on your own, hopefully this book will help you with the basics.

Now an important thing to remember as a female golfer is that we are never going to swing it like a male golfer. We are built completely different and because of that we are going to swing it differently. For example, women tend to be a lot more flexible, which means it's harder to keep the club in certain positions (you will find a lot of ladies on a full swing will overswing).

So please don't ever compare your swing to that of a man, or in fact any other woman. We are all unique which means that our golf swings are also going to be unique, which I like to think of as a wonderful thing.

So, what is most important to learn when starting golf...

Learn the short shots

This is one thing I wish I had been told earlier on in my golfing journey. You should spend at least half (I honestly would say 70%) of your practice time with your wedges and your putter. I know a lot of people love to go on the range and hit balls, and find short game practice boring, but it is so essential in improving your scores. Also, these days there are so many different challenges you can set yourself when practicing (see the golf games at the end of the book for some ideas), which can make things a little interesting & fun.

YouTube golf is not always helpful

If like me you have a golf obsessed partner, you will know that there is a lot of information out there. YouTube, Instagram, Twitter, you name it, there are golf tips everywhere! Now unlike the typical male (do not tell them I said that), your best option is to not try to copy everything you see online. Most of the tip videos you see on social media are accurate, however they are not always relevant to your own swing/game. For example, you wouldn't go into a pharmacy and buy every medicine on offer, if you only had a headache. You would buy the paracetamol to fix your head and that would be it. It is the same with golf, you only need to work on what is relevant to your problem. Plus, if you are trying too many different things, you're going to end up feeling like a confused octopus during your swing and hitting the ball will feel like an impossible challenge.

When in doubt, take a step back

Golf can really get you thinking too much, I mean to the point where you suddenly find yourself holding your breath because you are so focused on your golf shot. Over-thinking leads to tension, which is never good for the golf swing and the more you stress the harder golf becomes. Of course, it's hard to control your emotions and honestly sometimes golf can be the most frustrating thing in the world, but, whenever it gets to that point just take a step back and go back to your basics.

(See the chapter on psychology for some great stress relieving techniques)

Pre-Shot routine

Whenever you are on the range, try to resist the temptation to just hit shot after shot, as this isn't realistic to playing the game of golf. What I would like you to do instead, is create yourself a pre-shot routine that you are going to do before every shot. Every golfer that plays will have their own personalised version of this, however let me go through mine to show you an example.

- two practice swings
- walk behind the ball to choose my target
- walk back to ball and set myself up
- Breathe out
- Swing

A pre shot routine is put in place to keep you consistent, which in turn helps you to keep calm. We all know routine in life keeps our mentality steady, and it is no different with golf.

The do´s and don'ts

Do practice whenever you can. The only way we can improve our game is through repetition & learning the right things.

Dont just go and "whack balls"! Whoever said practice makes perfect was incorrect because practice, in fact, makes permanent. If you are going to the range & practicing the wrong things, you are only going to install bad habits into your game.

Do keep your eye on the ball. It is so important even when thinking about where you want to swing the club, that you are always keeping your eye on the ball. Look away and your rhythm and connection are gone.

Don't "keep your head down"! You will always get people telling you to keep your head down if you've hit a bad shot, but please ignore this advice! This action will only hinder your swing more. What you tend to see when someone "keeps their head down" is that they are then so fixated on doing just that, they forget to move their body or transfer their weight at all, which then leads to behind the ball ground hits or flicking arms and hands.

And…….

NEVER Listen to any male help ;)

Before we go any further, this is rule number one for me, to an extent...

One of my biggest tips for ladies who are learning golf or actually any women who play the game is NEVER listen to any males trying to help you with your golf (unless they are a golf coach or have read the MANuscript at the end of this book...)

The men in our lives, whether that be fathers, husbands, boyfriends, or brothers will only be trying to help, but, normally their delivery isn't the best. I mean remember when your dad taught you to drive, how it always ended in tears & arguments, well golf is no different.

The number of things I have witnessed over the years is enough to make any lady run for the hills when it comes to playing the game. From seeing husbands standing on the range with their arms crossed shouting at their wives "No, you're doing it wrong" or "why can't you do it" to telling them "They know best", when they then proceed to hit their own balls in every single direction but straight... I have had ladies' husbands give them the worst, most inaccurate information when most of the time they can't even get themselves around a golf course.

I once had one lady call me to tell me that her husband wanted to come to her lesson with her, so he could tell me what she was doing wrong. This was when I came up with the rule that no men are allowed to be around

when I am teaching any ladies. The new meaning for golf
– GIRLS ONLY, LADS FORBIDDEN...

I mean today literally as this book is about to be finished,
I endured what I can only describe as a mind-blowing
moment. I was teaching my ladies group class when the
lady on the end was suddenly approached by a man on
the range. He literally took the club out of her hands and
told her "This is how you are supposed to grip it".
Honestly, I couldn't believe my eyes and soon went over
to tell him thank you, but his unsolicited advice was not
needed. The poor lady felt so uncomfortable and said
that it happens to her regularly when she goes to the
range alone. The worst part is he was waiting to have a
lesson with one of the other teaching professionals, and
the shots I witnessed him hitting were not to be desired.

Unfortunately, this behaviour happens way to often and
it needs to stop, but here's what to do if you encounter
any unsolicited advice. If you have someone come over
who is about to offer you some help, try to shut it down
as soon as possible by being polite yet firm. "Thank you
so much for your advice, but I am doing okay on my
own". Do not ever let anyone make you feel
uncomfortable or that you are not good enough. Its
these events happening that really fuelled the fire for me
in writing this book.
Now as I mentioned before I know that not all men are
like that, and that in fact the men in our lives really are

only trying to help us. Which is why at the end of this book I have come up with the "MANuscript".

This is going to be a cut out page you can give to your partner to make sure he understands how to help guide you & support you through your journey in golf.

Chapter 6

From the Range to the Course

Throughout my career I have found that many ladies find that this is the biggest jump to make in terms of their golf development and journey. This isn't because they haven't acquired the skills needed, but mentally they find it the biggest hurdle to overcome.

I am here to tell you that YOU CAN DO IT!!

The Golf Course

So, first of all let's talk about the golf course itself! A regular course is made up of 18 holes, which consists of par 3, par 4 and par 5 holes to make up usually a total of Par 72 (This can range between 69-73).

The "par" of the hole is the number of shots a player should take to complete the hole. Therefore, the total par is the number of shots we are aiming to take to play the 18 holes.

Many people find that once they are having to think about a score, they get way too stressed out, and this is where the unhappy golf comes from. So, my advice is that until you are feeling comfortable on a golf course, just go and enjoy getting used to the course without worrying about how many shots you are taking.

The Scorecard

Now, for those who want to keep track of your scores, we have the scorecard. This is individual to each course, but the standard layout will be the same. Let's take a look at the basics of the card…

COMPETITION								ENTRY NO.			PLEASE INDICATE WHICH TEE USED
DATE						MEMB. NO.	HANDICAP		STROKES REC'D	PAR 70 SSS 70	
PLAYER A										PAR 70 SSS 09	
PLAYER B										PAR 73 SSS 73	

MARKER'S SCORE	HOLE	NAME	WHITE YARDS	YELLOW YARDS	PAR	SI	PLAYERS A	B	NETT SCORE	W = + L = - H = 0 POINTS	LADIES YARDS	PAR	SI
	1	LA VISTA	435	428	4	3					419	5	5
	2	THE PARKS	381	363	4	11					354	4	11
	3	CLAY PITS	188	182	3	13					174	3	13
	4	LOWER SLANG	534	530	5	5					445	5	3
	5	LITTLE WHITEMOOR	351	345	4	17					340	4	17
	6	GREENSFIELD	300	278	4	7					272	4	7
	7	ROUGH OAKS	356	312	4	9					298	4	9
	8	BESSIES BURROW	159	152	3	15					147	3	15
	9	HAWKS NEST	433	431	4	1					395	5	1
		OUT	3137	3021	35						2844	37	

PLEASE AVOID SLOW PLAY AT ALL TIMES

	10	LAKEVIEW	389	385	4	2					377	4	2
	11	AMBLEDOWN	305	297	4	10					267	4	10
	12	THREE OAKS	169	162	3	14					158	3	14
	13	THE HORSESHOE	276	270	4	16					262	4	12
	14	PEDDIMORE	495	486	5	6					437	5	6
	15	THE BELL	140	135	3	18					130	3	18
	16	THE PADDOCK	349	342	4	8					337	4	8
	17	DOUBLE UP	225	218	3	12					203	4	16
	18	FOX COVERT	504	470	5	4					425	5	4
		IN	2852	2765	35						2616	36	
		OUT	3137	3021	35						2844	37	
		TOTAL	5989	5786	70						5460	73	

			HANDICAP					Holes Won...........
	STABLEFORD POINTS OR PAR RESULT		NETT					Holes Lost.............
								Result.................

Marker's Signature _____   Player's Signature _____

Print Name _____   Print Name _____

Competition: Where you will write down the type of competition if you are playing one.

Handicap: Where you will write down your handicap, if you have one.

Player A: The name of the player this card belongs too.

Marker's score: In golf, you will never mark your own card, but instead your playing partners. The markers section is for you to write down your own scoring.

Hole number & Name – Which hole we are playing, and the name of that hole.

White yards: Distance of the hole from the men´s competition tee

Yellow yards: Distance of the hole from the men´s regular tee

Ladies' yards: Distance of the hole from the ladies tee.

Par: This is the target score for each hole. Total par is the target score for the whole 18 holes.

SI: This is the stroke index. Each hole is ranked from easiest to hardest. 1 being the most difficult & 18 being the least difficult.

Total Score: All your scores from the 18 holes added up.

Nett score: Your score minus your handicap.

Stableford points: We will come to in the next chapter.

First time to the course advice

Start small – Golf is hard enough without taking on a monster course as your first attempt, and in most areas you will find either a par 3 course, or a smaller 9-hole course. These are usually better options to begin playing on before trying an 18-hole championship course, as it will ease you in nicely and not put you off golf forever. Also, by building yourself up slowly you can build your game's stamina and consistency. I first started on this little pitch and putt course, with overgrown grass, bald golf mats and broken flags, but wow did I enjoy it. It really helped me to build up my game and confidence right in the very beginning of learning.

Choose a late tee time – Playing later in the day means that there will not be as many other golfers on the course. There is nothing worse than added pressure because the course is full & the group behind is constantly on your tail. I still now feel the anxiety when the group behind is literally standing & waiting, and I hate it (for some reason there are a few people who think that it is a race around the course, and it is one of my serious pet hates!) So, by playing later in the day, you will avoid these Speedy Gonzalez golfers, and enjoy a round at your own pace. Also, it is in our human nature to worry about other people around us, so playing later will take away any stress you may feel about "holding people up" or "being a pain".

Never fear playing golf – just learn the general golf etiquette

I know that it can be so daunting heading out onto the course, and you probably feel like you're not supposed to be out there, or you don't know what you're doing. I promise you though, that once you know the basic etiquette, there is no reason for any lady to feel like they aren't equipped enough.

- Learn the basic Rules of Golf
  - Keep the pace
  - Wait your turn
  - Know where to stand
  - Watch other people's lines
  - Take care of the course
  - What to wear

Learn the Basic Rules of Golf

Let me tell you, there are many, many rules in golf and sometimes you don't even know about one until you are in the scenario out on the course. (I have found myself many times confused by what the heck I'm supposed to do, and that's after a lot of years of golfing). However, there is a R&A rules book that you are allowed to keep in your golf bag for any ruling situations you need help with.

For now, let's go through the basic everyday rules you might need to know, when you are first heading out onto the course.

Equipment

Clubs: You can carry a maximum of 14 clubs. If you have an extra club in your bag that you practice with leave it in the car to avoid complications. The 14 clubs can be a combination of anything you like.

Ball: You must finish a hole with the same ball you started it with. You can change your ball between holes but not during a hole. The only exception is if you lose a ball during a hole (you can use any other ball from your bag and the new ball becomes "in play.")

Tee Box

You must tee the ball up behind the "line" created by the two tee markers, and you can place it as far back as the length of two drivers. The main point to remember is never in front of the tee markers, as this is classed as an advantage. Lady golfers will generally start off the forward tee boxes out on the course.

Order of play

For the shot off the tee, order of play is determined by the score from the previous hole. This means that the lowest scorer hits first, and then the next lowest goes next until everyone has hit. During the hole itself the order of play is based on who is furthest away from the hole.

The exception to this rule, is if you and your friends want to play 'ready golf'. This type of golf is where whoever is ready to go hits their ball first, regardless of their score on the previous hole, or their distance from the pin. I find this the best way to play golf because it keeps your round flowing.

During the hole

-The golden rule is you must play the ball as it lies. This means that you are not allowed to move the ball to a better position (Unless there is "placing lies" on the course), or try to improve your lie by altering the ground around the ball. Also, as much as we would like to, the breaking or bending of branches to allow you to swing easier at the ball is unfortunately not allowed.

-When you are in a bunker always remember that you cannot ground the club in the sand behind, or in front of the ball before playing your shot. Also, as well as the club you are not allowed to test the consistency of the sand with the likes of your hands, feet or the rake. (However, a little tip is that when you wiggle your feet in the sand to lower yourself for your bunker shot, use this to get a little feel of the sand)

-If you hit your ball into a water hazard, then you will have to drop your ball and take a penalty shot. Sometimes however, you may get lucky and there may be no water in the hazard. If this is the case, then you can play out of it using the same rules as if it were a bunker shot. (No grounding the club or moving any loose impediments like leaves or stones.)

-You can't place anything in front of your ball for aiming at.

-You are allowed to pick up sticks, stones, leaves, rocks, boulders, feathers, dead grass and pine needles that are around your ball but make sure you do not move the ball while doing so, otherwise you will receive a penalty shot. It has happened to me before because I am such a klutz, and I can't tell you how annoyed at myself I was.

Lost ball

You have 3 minutes to find a lost ball, otherwise you must go back to your previous spot and re-hit the shot with a penalty stroke added.
(Unless you have hit a "provisional ball", in which you

then carry on with that ball down the hole, with a one-shot penalty)

Free drops

-You may drop away from temporary water on the surface of the ground that is not marked as a hazard.
-You may drop away from areas marked GUR - Ground Under Repair.

Putting & on the green

- First of all, make sure you keep all trolleys & golf bags off the putting green surface.
- You are allowed to move stones, sand, gravel, leaves and other loose items that land on your line between your ball and the hole. To move these items, you may pick or use the back of your hand to brush them away, but you are not allowed to "stroke" the grass with the palm of your hand.

-You are allowed to fix indents on the putting green made either by ball pitch marks, or shoe spikes.

-Sometimes your ball maker may be in the way of your playing partners line & they may ask you to move it to the left or right. To do this place the heel of the putter head next to the marker and move the marker to the toe of the putter. (Always remember to replace the marker to the original position before you play your putt)

-Sometimes your ball may stop right on the edge of the hole. If this happens you are allowed to wait 10 seconds to see if it drops in. (One of the most infuriating scenarios in golf)

Keep the Pace

So, in this game you are going to have holes where absolutely nothing will go right, and it happens to beginners and to seasoned golfers. My advice firstly would be that if this happens, just keep going. Get to your ball, have a practice swing, and give it a rip!

If you start to feel too overwhelmed or stressed though, just pick up your ball and move onto the next hole. There is literally nothing wrong with doing this when you are learning to play. Also, you can let the group behind through if you are worried about holding them up.

Other good tips to keeping the pace, is to make sure that you leave your bag/ trolley on the side of the green where you will be exiting towards the next tee. For example, if the next tee is right of the green you are currently playing, leave your bag on the right side. Also wait until the next tee box to fill in your scorecard as opposed to doing it on the green, in case the people behind are waiting to hit their shots.

Wait your turn

When you are playing down the hole always be aware of your playing partners, and make sure that you wait your turn. Trust me there is nothing worse than when you are in the zone, ready to swing and you suddenly hear your playing partner strike a shot. You lose all the build-up and readiness that you had achieved for your shot. I have played with many guys who do this (you know men, they tend to lack awareness of their surroundings) so just be mindful of your playing partners.

Waiting your turn applies even more so if you have decided to play "ready golf", as obviously without any order, anyone can play their shot next. To avoid this happening, just check with your partners "shall I go", before hitting your shot.

Know where to stand

I feel like this is one of the things that brings the fear when being on the golf course! That feeling of, "dear god where do I stand so I am not in the way". Now, I would say that except for a couple of places, the golf course is all yours, but let's go through the main places to avoid standing;

Infront of someone – This one is kind of self-explanatory in the sense of we obviously do not want to get hit on the head by a golf ball or be in someone's line.

(Also, when you are on the putting green make sure you are not directly in front of someone or in their eye line, as this can be very distracting or off putting – for example don't stand behind the hole)

Standing behind someone's back – Again this relates to you not getting hit whilst they are swinging, but also it can make the person playing their shot feel uneasy and cautious.

Watch other people's lines

This is mostly aimed at your playing partners lines on the putting green, because with this shot our ball rolls along the floor, and can therefore be affected by any indentations on the surface, aka your footprint! When walking on the putting green, be aware of where your playing partners balls & ball markers are so you don't accidentally walk across their line. The best way to avoid someone's putting line is to walk around the back of the marker/ ball, however the split leg jump across their line is always a useful technique to learn too! So, when you have seen golfers on a green walking in weird directions and doing the splits this is what they are doing.

Take care on the course

Being hit by a golf ball can hurt, a lot! Please always be aware of where you are walking.

If you hit it offline (like most of us do, don't worry this is very normal) Just yell "fore" to keep others on the course safe. Also, if you hear the shout whilst you're on the course, I suggest ducking down and putting your hands on your head for protection. I bet you never knew golf was such a thrill-seeking sport!

What to Wear

Women's golf clothing has changed a lot since I first began playing (there are some photos that will never again see the light of day), and thankfully these days there is a lot more choice for women to wear.

Back in the day I was always told off for not wearing the right shoes in the clubhouse, or for my skirt being too short out on the course (whoops), but like I said luckily the ladies' game has moved on into a better direction. Most courses will have their own set of golf attire "rules" and you will find some clubs are more relaxed with theirs than others. However, you can never go wrong by wearing a polo shirt and some trousers/ shorts. Collarless shirts and leggings are now also becoming popular clothing items that are acceptable to wear on the course too.

Chapter 7
First competition

Handicaps

Each player's handicap is a measure of the number of extra shots over par that they are expected to take on a course. Players with a 'higher' handicap will be allowed a higher number of extra strokes over the course par. Players with a 'low' handicap are expected to take fewer additional strokes to get around the course.

As an amateur, a handicap allows you to play golf against any other player, of any skill level and on any course, with a reasonable chance of competing against each other fairly.

Playing your first competition

So, not everyone may want to play competitive golf and that is fine, there is no rule that you must play competitions if you don't want to.
However, for those of you who do want to, maybe club or society comps, hopefully this chapter of the book will help you to prepare.

My first competition

Even to this day I can remember my very first competition that I played in. I was only 9 years old, and it was called the "five counties jamboree". The competition was only 6 holes long and was specifically for junior golfers. Long story short, I only ended up going and winning the whole thing!! Now of course I don't want this to make you feel like you must go and win your first ever competition, but instead I wanted to show you that my first event was literally only 6 holes. I don't think I had a full 18-hole competition until maybe a full year later.

Enjoy Yourself!

The most important thing to remember when you go to play a competition, is to enjoy yourself! The more relaxed you can be going into playing a competitive round, the more fun you will have and the better you will play. You almost need to go with no expectations. This may sound like the most negative comment ever; however, it is something you need to remember.

Know the format

Now, within golf there are so many different formats that can be played when it comes to competitions, and all of these formats can be played seriously, or be played to have a bit of fun with your friends. You will find that a lot of golf clubs will have their weekly & annual championship competitions, but they will also have some fun competitions too. I have so many great memories as a junior playing some of these fun events with my dad, sister, and friends at the time. Well, I say "fun", but I have always been super competitive whatever the competition may be, I just cant help it.

I am going to go through each of these different formats now..

Strokeplay

Strokeplay is the most common form of competition that you will find played in competitions. In stroke play, every player (or team) competes all 18 holes and counts the total number of strokes they have on each hole. This is classed as the "gross score". There is also normally a winner of the "nett score" which is the total score less the player's handicap.

Stableford

Stableford is a form of strokeplay, however the scoring is made by points awarded in relation to the par of each hole. It is a great game for beginners & high handicappers because you can mess up a hole or two, but still be in with a chance to win the competition.

Hole Played in Points;
< than 1 over par = 0 points
1 over Par = 1 points
Par = 2 points
1 under par = 3 points
2 under par = 4 points
3 under par = 5 points

According to your handicap a player may receive 1 or 2 shots per hole. Aka if you play off 36 you will receive 2 shots per hole, for example;

Par: 4
Score: 6
Shots: 2
Nett Score: 4
Points: 2

36 points is a player playing to "their handicap" but the winner of the competition is the player who scores the highest number of points.

Scramble

Each player in a team (of two, three or four players) tees off on each hole and the players then decide between them which shot was the best. Once this has been decided, the other players will then pick up their balls and play their second shot from that position. This carries on for every shot until the hole is finished.

*Once you have chosen the ball you wish to play, use a tee peg/or marker to mark the spot for the other players. They must then place their ball within one scorecard's width of the selected position, or when you are on the putting green within one putter head from the marker.

Matchplay

In match play, two players (or two teams) play every hole as a separate contest against each other. The player(s) with the lower score wins the hole, regardless of how many shots that player took versus par.

If the scores of both players or teams are equal, the hole is "halved" (drawn). If a player wins a hole they will go "1 up" and from this can either go "2 up" if they win the next hole or "all square" if the opponent wins the next hole. This continues until someone wins (aka 5 up with only 4 holes left to play), or if the game finishes all square on the 18th hole.

Matchplay is an extremely popular form of competition at club level & personally is my favourite game, because as I have previously said I am a teeny, little bit competitive. Golf is a very solo sport, so when you get the chance to play a matchplay game for a team, there is nothing more exciting. There is a competition played by the women professionals called the Solheim Cup which you should definitely watch. It is Europe vs USA and makes for some great golf watching.

Fourball betterball

This format is played as a team event, however each player in the team plays with their own ball, but at the end of the hole the better score of the team counts. Fourball betterball can be played as either match play or stroke play.

Foursomes

Foursomes is similar to fourball betterball, however it is played between two players in partnership, meaning they play one ball between them, which they hit alternately. For example, one player tees off, and then the other shots are played in turns until the hole is finished. (Penalty shots do not affect the order of play.)

This game again can be played under match play or stroke play rules.

Keep fuelled

When you are playing golf always make sure that you are hydrated, and eating well during your round. If we lose our energy levels, this can lead to poor decision making and fatigue towards the end of the round. You know when your hangry and your mind doesn't make any sense? Well, try playing golf when you're feeling like that!
My go to on the course is a bottle of water, Lucozade and a mixed food bag of goodies.
You will be able to check out all on course nutrition in Chapter 8.

Attitude of Gratitude

Golf is a privilege not an entitlement. Whether it's the family fun event, the Sunday medal or the final round of the Club Championships, a shift in your perspective can really help take some pressure off yourself. Be grateful for the opportunity to be out there playing the beautiful game, as there are worser things that you could be doing. Enjoy it and embrace the rollercoaster ride that is golf.

Chapter 8
On course Nutrition

Keeping fuelled on the course is an important part of golf, that many people don't tend to think of. Back in the day, well when I first started playing golf, I used to always mess up on the last 4 holes of my round consistently. It took my dad and I a while to realise that it was because I was so mentally & physically burnt out by the end of the round, that I literally had no energy left to function. Soon after we started really looking into the nutrition side of golf, and how to keep my energy levels high for the full 18 holes. I'm going to share with you a few of my favourite snacks that kept me going during my rounds.

Food

Trail Mix

If you want a great golf snack that's high in protein and long-lasting energy, trail mix is the way to go. Not only are there a variety of organic trail mix brands to choose from, but you can easily make your own trail mix at home. All you need is your favourite type of nuts, some chocolate, and dried fruit, and you have the perfect golf snack.

I used to like to make my own using dried cranberries, cashew nuts, almonds, corn kernels & a little sprinkle of salt.

Fresh Fruit

Fresh fruit is a great way to supplement any golfer's snack pack. Fruits are high in carbs and nutrients that give you a natural energy boost. However, be careful of fruits that are high in sugar as they could spike your energy levels throughout the day. Bananas are one of my favourite on course fruit snacks, because they provide long lasting energy and contain a protein that helps create serotonin in our brain, which in turn keeps us happy!

Nuts

Not into dried fruit and chocolate? Skip the trail mix and go with some simple mixed nuts. Not only are they easy to tuck into your golf bag, but they will keep you full and energized throughout the game.

Granola Bars

Granola bars are another reliable, tasty snack to stash in your golf bag. You can get them at the store or make your own at home for an even healthier option.

My little trick is that I like to break them up into 18 pieces and make sure that I have a piece on every tee shot. This was because I felt I could maintain a consistent level of energy throughout the round

Peanut butter and Jelly (jam) Sandwich
(Can you tell I lived in America?)
Exactly what it says in the title. Peanut butter and jam on a sandwich! The best thing you can do is cut these sandwiches into quarters and try to eat one quarter every 2-3 holes to maintain blood sugar and stay energized.

Drink

Water
Drinking water keeps your mind and body working properly and it's critical for optimal brain function and muscle performance. Being dehydrated by just 2-3% results in 10% lower performance which in an average round of golf, could be as high as 8 shots!

Lucozade/ Isotonic drink
Isotonic drinks contain similar concentrations of salt and sugar as in the human body. Therefore, these drinks quickly replace fluids lost through sweating and supplies a boost of carbohydrates to your body. This makes them a great fluid to take out on the course with you to keep you surviving playing on the course.

Chapter 9

Golf Psychology

Golf, as is life, is very much a game played in the head. The mental side to golf needs just as much attention & development as the practical side, if not more! (One thing I work so hard on myself). You will find that the hardest distance to control when out on the course, is the distance between your ears haha.

Golf is obviously a sport that is very individual, which means you cannot really rely on others to help get you through it. It's just you and that little voice inside your head out there, which is why we need to make sure that they become best friends.

It can sometimes be very hard to keep your head calm out on the course, however there are a few different techniques you can use to keep yourself happy & positive.

I now want to go through with you, the different methods that I have learnt over the years to help keep my mental space a place of peace, rather than chaos.

Psychology tips for the course

Breathing

My advice on this it to breathe out before you play your shot. Honestly this is a technique that has helped myself and my students hugely in playing successful golf shots. The worst thing for your golf swing is to be uptight, yet by holding your breath while you swing all you are going to do is tense & tighten your whole body.

So, before each shot let out a nice big breath to allow your body to relax so that you are all set for a nice smooth swing.

Positive self-talk

This is something that again is to be said for life, and not just golf. Talking to yourself positively is the best way to get your mind into a happy, calm state.

Positive self-talk makes you feel good about yourself and the things that are going on in your life. It's like having an optimistic voice in your head that always looks on the bright side. Examples.

"I can do anything I put my mind to"

"I can totally make this shot"

It might not seem like much, but self-talk is a huge part of building our self-esteem and confidence. By working on replacing negative self-talk with more positive self-talk, you're more likely to feel in control of the things going on around you (and your golf game)

Keep your head high

Something my dad told me when I was younger was to always "Look to the top of the tallest tree". This was to make sure that I was keeping my head held high and staying positive. It really is amazing how your body language can affect your mood. I mean if you are walking round staring at your feet or the ground, you can tend to walk yourself into a little bit of a mental hole. There is a reason that we say, "keep your chin up", and this is because it helps to promote a more confident/ positive mentality.

Find peace on the course.

When you practice hard and admit to yourself that you really want to play well, it's easy to build up your round into something so huge that you can't play. You can become so panicked that you get yourself so tied up in knots suddenly up feels like down. The golf course must be your sanctuary, somewhere you love, and a place where you are not afraid to mess up. Once you can find a level of inner peace, and just appreciate being out on the course, you will find golf becomes easier.

Don't be seduced by results
This means stop allowing yourself to be seduced by a score or by winning until you have finished your round. Sometimes we can get to ahead of ourselves that we forget to focus on the moment in front of us. I have done it, and not just once, and it really is the best way to ruin a round ha. I can remember one time where I had played 17 holes without making a bogey and I was so excited as I had never had a bogey free round before. On the 18th hole, which was a par 3 hole, I had played my ball to the middle of the green off the tee, and in my head I had already finished. Well, I'm sure you can guess what happened, I went on to three putt from 15 feet away and made a bogey!! So always make sure that you are focusing on the process and execution of the shot in front of you. "One shot at a time" being the key statement to remember. Always remain in the present.

The past is the past

As well as not getting seduced by future results, also make sure that you leave what has already happened behind you. Again, just like in life we cannot change the things in the past, therefore we are wasting our energy by giving them our thoughts. If you have a bad shot, or a bad hole, leave it behind you and keep calm and carry on as they say.

Every shot is a new challenge

If you go into a golf round knowing that every shot is unique, and that you are going to have good ones & bad ones, you will find that you put much less pressure on yourself. Each time you reach your ball it is a new opportunity to play a good shot. Enjoy the challenge of trying to see how good you can make that one shot, without worrying about the outcome of the rest of the hole.

Keep a routine

When you are out on the course it is important to keep the same mental and physical routine with every shot that you play. This will help to keep you focused on what you have to do and the process, so that when the pressure is on it helps you manage your nerves. Create a pre-shot routine that works for you and stick with it.

Quiet the eyes

In the movie Bagger Vance (a great golf film with Will Smith & Matt Damon that you should definitely watch) he states, "you can't look at that flag as some dragon you've got to slay, you need to look with soft eyes". The basic underlying meaning of this is stop trying to kill the ball ha! You're going to find in golf that the more frustrated you get or the harder you try the game becomes even harder to play. Now like I have said many times in this book, I know golf can be frustrating, but when you're out on that course the more you can keep a positive mindset (even when its going wrong) the more you will enjoy the game & play better.

Expectations

Ryan Reynolds said, "When you have expectations, you are setting yourself up for failure" and this couldn't be truer with golf. We should all set ourselves goals for our game, but we should never "expect" to shoot a certain score or play a certain way. In golf sometimes you can get good breaks from bad shots, and bad breaks from good shots, and nothing is promised to you. Of course the more we practice, the higher our odds are that we will play better, but always try to manage your expectations, as it really helps to keep the pressure off of yourself. I've always found that I play better golf when I am kind to myself and release the expectations that I SHOULD be doing something.

Never give up

Be a fighter! In my opinion golf is one of the hardest mentally challenging sports out there and it is so easy to become demoralised and want to give up. I can tell you though there is nothing more satisfying than breaking through a rough patch and coming out on the other side. The pride you feel in yourself is something that you can take with you into life.

Switch off between shots

When you are walking between your shots, I want you to think of everything else but golf. Before and after every shot you need to have a "trigger" that puts you in and takes you out of "golf mode". For me this is soon as I put my glove on to take a shot or take my glove off after each shot. I had a rule with my dad that we weren't allowed to discuss anything golfing in between playing my shots, and instead would talk about the weather, life, but most of the time food ha!

Sing your favourite tune

Now this is a technique I have used so much myself in the past, to the point where sometimes my dad would laugh at me because unbeknown to me, I was actually singing out loud while playing my shot ha! Sometimes your brain can get really overrun by so many different thoughts, and its overwhelming. I have always found that if I am singing my favourite song in my head, it not only drowns out the thoughts, but also makes me feel a lot calmer.

BELIEVE IN YOU

My final psychology thought I want you to have, which is the most important part to remember, is to believe in yourself! My motto is the more you believe, the more you become, so if we want to succeed we have to have the faith and belief in ourself.
I am a BIG believer in the law of attraction, and that our thoughts become our reality, and it was Descartes himself who said "I think, therefore I am". Our minds are

SO strong and we need to make sure we are feeding them with positivity to be able to manifest the things that we want.

Chapter 10

Golf Lesson Chat

Do you have a lesson and sometimes think what on earth are you talking about? The terms your golf professional is throwing at you sounds like some form of quantum psychics equation that makes no sense at all! Well, hopefully this section can help...

Alignment: This is the relationship of the feet, shoulders, and club face to the target you are aiming at.

Angle of attack: This is the measurement of how steep or shallow the clubhead is moving relative to the ground through impact. It can be negative (hitting down on the ball) or positive (hitting up on the ball)

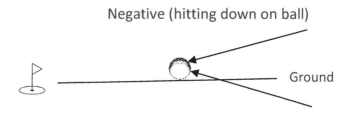

Negative (hitting down on ball)

Ground

Positive (hitting up on ball)

Ball flights: 9 different flights the ball can take;

Straight: Lands on target line.

Fade: Starts left of target line, curves right and lands on target.

Draw: Starts right of target line, curves left and lands on target.

Pull: This is when the ball starts left of the target and flies without any curvature, landing left of the target.

Push: This is when the ball starts right of the target and flies without any curvature, landing right of the target.

Slice: This is when the ball starts left of the target, curves a lot to the right, and finishes right of the target.

Hook: This is when the ball starts right of the target, curves a lot to the left, and finishes left of the target.

Pull Hook: This is when the ball starts left of the target, curves even more to the left, and lands very left of the target.

Push Slice: This is when the ball starts right of the target, curves even more to the right, and lands very right of the target.

Back-swing: This is the initiation of the swing by taking the club from behind the ball to behind your head.

Breaking your wrists too early (early release): This is when you have released your wrist before striking the ball. (The clubhead is in front of your hands at impact) When this happens, we lose connection and compression on the golf ball and normally leads to a poor strike.

Carry: This is the distance that the ball flies in the air before hitting the ground.

Closed Stance: This is when your feet are aiming right of the target at set up.

Clubface: The surface on the head of a golf club used to hit the ball.

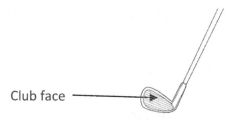

Club face

Club path: This is the direction that the club is going through impact - either straight, left, or right.

Clubhead Speed: Club Speed is the speed the club head is traveling immediately prior to impact.

Closed clubface: When you hit a shot but the club face at impact is pointing to the left of the target line as a right-handed player.

Compression / compress the ball: This is the force that we put onto the ball to create the power & distance of the shot.

Decelerate: This is when we see a decrease in the club head speed near to impact

Downswing: This is the moving of the club from the top of the swing toward the ball for impact.

Follow-through: This is the part of the swing that ends the swing sequence and is after impact position.

Heel of the club: This is the part of the club head closest to you, where the shaft enters the club head.

Heel

Holding it off: This is when we don't allow the golf club to naturally release through the impact of the ball.

Hosel: The part of the club where the shaft attaches to the clubhead.

Hitting up on the ball: This is us hitting with a positive angle of attack (upwards). We should only hit up on the ball when playing a driver shot.

Hitting down on the ball: This is us hitting with a negative angle of attack. Shots hit off the ground should always have a negative attack angle to give us the trajectory and lift we need.

Lifting your head: This is when you prematurely look up to see where the ball is going which often results in poor shots, especially topping the ball.

In-to-out: The clubhead path travels from the inside of the target line to the outside as it impacts the ball.

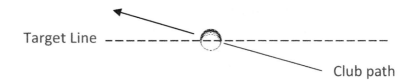

Target Line

Club path

Impact: The moment when the club strikes the ball!

Lie of the club: This is the angle formed between the shaft and the line of the ground when the clubhead is resting on the ground.

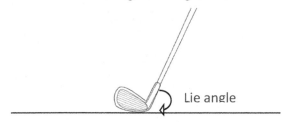

Lie angle

Leading edge: The leading edge is located at the bottom of the clubface. It is the part of the club where the sole meets the clubface.

Leading edge

Open Clubface: When you hit a shot but the club face at impact is pointing to the right of the target line as a right-handed player.

Open stance: This is when your feet are aiming left of the target line at set up.

Out-to-in: The clubhead path travels from the outside of the target line to the inside as it impacts the ball.

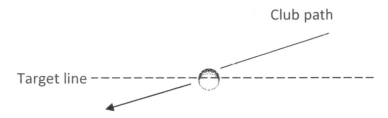

Posture: This is the position we put our body into at set up.

Pre-shot routine: The practice swings and movements golfers make before they're about to hit. Try to create one for yourself to make a repeatable routine to get comfortable but make it efficient.

Release: This refers to the flow of the arms and body through the ball. To fully release the golf club, you want to swing through impact and allow the club to naturally turn and rotate with your body, letting the toe of the clubhead point up to the sky after you've hit the ball.

Set up –There are several key elements in the golf setup such as proper alignment, the correct stance and ball position, good posture, and a functional grip.

Sweet spot: The area on the club face that surrounds the centre of the clubface where the most distance will be produced on your shots. (The spot that when you hit it makes a sound that tingles your whole-body ha)

Transferring your weight: This is the movement of your weight throughout the golf swing. (One of the most important aspects of a golf swing)

Toe of the club: The end of the club face furthest from the hosel.

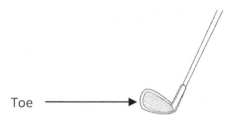

Toe

Chapter 11

Golf Terms

Par: This is the number of strokes you should take to finish the hole.

Birdie: One under par.
Eagle: Two under par.

Albatross: Three under par.
Bogey: one over par.

Double bogey: two over par.

Triple bogey: three over par.

Above the hole: This refers to the position of your ball on the putting green when your next putt is playing down the hill towards the hole.

Approach shot: This is the shot you are hitting with the intention of landing it on the green. This can range from a wedge through to a wood on any par 4 or 5.

Attending the flag: This is when a player holds and removes the flag for another player who is putting. "Could you tend that for me please"

Ball marker: This is something you will need to mark the position of your ball when lifting it on the green to either clean it or remove your ball out of the way of your playing partners. (There are so many glitzy ball markers you can get these days too, don't be like me and just use a €1 coin ha)

Below the hole: This refers to the position of your ball on the putting green when your next putt is playing up the hill to the hole.

Break: This is the movement of the ball left or right on the putting green due to the lay of the land. This is what we consider when we "read the green".

Bunker/ sand trap: I know us ladies love a good beach trip; however, this is one area of sand you want to avoid. These are sand filled pits of despair that you can find both down the sides of a fairway or guarding a green.

Caddie: This is the person who carries your clubs around the course for you. It is a luxury you may find at some courses; however, they are not a necessity.

Dog leg: This does not refer to your Dachshunds actual leg, but to a bend in the hole/fairway. This can be either to the left or the right, and sometimes makes the flag non-visible from the tee.

Downhill putt: This is when we are putting down a slope towards the hole. These putts tend to be much harder in judging your speed and aim.

Divot: This is the chunk of dirt that you take out of the ground from playing your golf shot after striking the ball.

This is usually from your irons or wedges (taking a divot with the driver is, how can I put this, not ideal haha)

Fairway: The mowed grass that leads you to the hole (the place you want to be)

Mud Ball: A devilish situation where mud has caked itself onto your golf ball making it nearly impossible to tell which direction it will go.

Fat/ chunk shot: This is when a shot takes a BIG divot out of the grass before the ball, which will limit the distance your ball flies. (You're playing partners are not referring to your bum when they say "that one looked a bit chunky")

Flyer: This usually happens from the rough when the grass gets between the club & ball, resulting in the ball flying way too far.

Fore: If you hear this, DUCK! Golfers will shout this when they hit their ball offline towards other golfers. You may hear fore left/ or right. Remember to always shout fore if you hit a wayward shot yourself, and don't be shy, shout it as loud as you can!

Green: This is the area of very finely mowed grass you will find at the end of the hole where the actual hole itself is.

Gimmie: This is when your ball has finished so close to the hole, it is pretty impossible to miss the next putt. A gimmie is only "officially" used in matchplay, however when playing for fun we tend to use these to help speed up play, and we "give" our playing partners putts the are close to the hole. "You can have that", "I will give you that" and "that's good" are all phrases you can hear for gimmie putts.

Grounding the club: This refers to your golf club in hazard situations. Letting your club head touch the surface of the ground, in water hazards and bunkers, is against the rules and will result in a penalty.

Gross: This is the number of shots you have taken to play around the course, without taking your handicap into account.

GUR (Ground under repair): This is an area on the course that is normally damaged or under maintenance, where the player is entitled to a free drop if their ball has landed in it. The area is normally identified with a sign, stakes or line.

Handicap: This is a number given to a player, based on their average golf scores, which is the amount over par a player should score. For example, if you're playing a course with a par 72, and your handicap is 30 then you are expected to shoot 102. The lower scores you shoot, the lower your handicap becomes.

Hazards: These are areas on the course that you wish a golf course didn't have. These include bunkers, ponds, lakes, ditches & anywhere that is outside the border of the golf course (out of bounds)

Hole in one: This is when you get your ball in the hole in one shot (mostly on par 3´s). This does incur a penalty though, of having to buy everyone in the bar a drink haha.

Honour: This is given to the player who scored the lowest on the last hole and is then granted to tee off first on the next hole.

Lie: This is the spot where the ball has come to rest (after playing your shot / before your next shot). Sometimes you can end up with a good lie like a fluffy piece of grass on the fairway, or a bad lie like ending up in someone else's divot.

Line (putting): This is the visualised path a ball should take on its way to the hole. Getting the line right by reading the green is important if you want to hole putts. Always be aware on the putting green of other people's "lines" so that you do not disturb/ or leave indentations, on the path their ball will take.

Line (full swing): "What's my line here?" Usually, you find your line by aiming at something behind where you want the ball to land and essentially creates a line between you and your target.

Mulligan: This is a free redo of your shot. A mulligan is not in the rule book of golf, however if you're playing for fun your friends may let you get away with one now and then.

Nett: This is your score when you have taken your handicap away from your gross score.

Out of Bounds: This is not a good place to be, but we all find it now and then. The area of out of bounds is normally shown by white posts and signifies the course boundaries.

Order of play: This is the order in which players in the group play their shots. Off the tee, you will play your shots in order of who got the lowest score on the previous hole. Down the rest of the hole, who goes next is determined by who is furthest away from the hole - "Furthest away is first to play."

Pin/ Flag: This is the target you aim at throughout the hole which indicates where the actual "hole" is on the green.

Pitch mark: This is the damage made to a green created by your ball landing on the soft ground. Always remember to repair your pitchmarks ladies, and any others you find where someone hasn't been so vigilant.

Provisional ball: This a second golf ball played by a golfer who believes their first ball (the stroke just played) may be lost.

Rough: These are areas of long grass that are either side of the fairway. Again, this is an area we don't want to be in, however regular visits are definitely the norm.

Ready golf: This is when the order of play is scrapped, and players take their shots based on who is ready to play. This way of golf is now highly popular as it helps groups to keep up with pace of play.

Stroke: Another way of describing the number of shots you have taken to get down the hole. It can also be used to refer to the putting "swing".

Shank: Just like the word Voldemort in Harry Potter, this shot is one that "must not be named". A shank (or a leg of lamb as I like to refer to it) is a shot that comes off the hosel of the club, nearly missing the club completely, resulting in a ball that shoots off wildly at right angles.

Tee Box: This is the designated area that marks the beginning of each hole. Most courses will use red markers to indicate the ladies tee.

Thin shot: This is when you hit the ball from low on the clubface and not quite out the "sweet spot". This results in a low "stinging" flight, stinging because these types of shots hurt your hands.

Topping the ball: This is when you hit the ball with the bottom of the club face, resulting in a shot that tends to "roll" not fly, seeing more ground than air. Reference *worm burner*

Three-putt: Exactly what it says on the box, this is when you take 3 putts instead of 2 (or 1) on the putting green. For me this is one of the most annoying things to do after playing tee to green beautifully as you can sometimes end up taking more putts than you have shots. (Hence the saying "drive for show, putt for dough")

Up & down: This is when you have one chip and one putt.

Funny golf terms to hold your own on the course..

Snowman – Making an 8 on a hole.

Bandit: This is someone who always plays better than their handicap.

Horseshoed – When the ball goes around the hole and comes back towards you.

On the dance floor – Hitting it on the putting green.

Worm killer/ worm burner – A close to the ground low shot.

Fried egg: This is a golf ball that is buried in a bunker.

There are no pictures on a scorecard – You may have played the ugliest shot in golf & got away with it, or had a hole filled with ugly shots yet still walked away with a par. However, golf is a game of scoring, so it doesn't really matter how you got it down the hole but how quickly!

The big dog – This is another name for your driver, "Let the big dog eat".

Ace – A hole in one.

Army golf – When you are hitting it left & right down the hole (left, left, left right left)

Giraffes Bum – Too high & it stinks (my dad made me put this one in, sorry)

19th hole – Aka the bar... A great place to wind down after your round.

UBU: A shot that is "ugly but useful".

Dead Sheep: When it is "Still ewe".

Chapter 12

Practice Games & Drills

Practice drills are a great way to make your practice more relatable to on course playing, and much more fun.

Truth be told I used to get bored quite easily practicing and I really am more of a "play on the course" golfer than a range dweller. However, I knew if I were to make any improvements to my game, and get better, I had to practice.

For me using drills and setting myself little challenges/ games really made my practice much more exciting and endurable.

In this chapter I have written down a few of my favourites for each different part of the game from Putting to Driving.

Putting

The Clock Drill

Pick one hole and place 12 tees around the hole 3 feet away. You're then going to work your way around the hole & see how long it takes for you to hole all the balls in a row!
Once you have holed all the balls all in a row, move all the tees back another foot and try again.

Putting around the clock will not only help you to practise your short putts, but also help you to improve your ability to read the break of different putts.

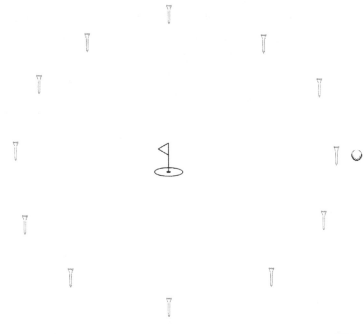

The Gate Drill

This is one of the most famous golf putting drills practiced by the pros.

So, you are going to measure out a putt 6 feet away from the hole and then set two tees about a putter head width apart (Gate #1). Then you are going to set two more tees (Gate #2) about a golf balls width apart and 3 feet in front of your first tee gate.

If both the putter and the ball pass through their respective gates, without making contact, it is counted a success.

Try to achieve 10 successful attempts or practice the skill for half an hour.

Putting through tracks

Another way to practice a straighter back, straighter through stroke is to use two clubs (or alignment rods). Place them outside the heel and the toe of your putter, place a ball in the middle and then putt through the lines. This helps you to work on keeping a more stable back and through motion with your putting stroke.

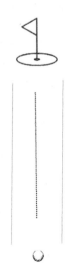

Pace putting target drill

This is a great distance-control drill that is perfect for those struggling with their pace.

You are going to need 6 tees which you are going to place in a semi-circle around the hole, 5 golf balls, and a starting distance of 20 feet away.

The aim is to achieve a score of 0 or better, with the points being;

- Minus 1 for a putt that ends up short or out of the tees
- 1 point for a ball that finishes within the tees
- 2 points for a ball that goes in the hole.

Once you have achieved this, bring your starting distance back an extra 5 feet.

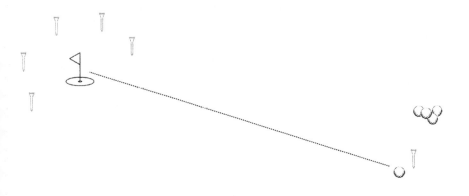

Distance control drill

This is another great practice game to work on your speed control.

The aim of this game is to try and get as many balls as you can in the 15-foot space.
You are going to play your first ball, and then with your second ball try to just hit it a little past the first ball. You are going to repeat this process until either you run out of space, or you don't hit the current ball past your last balls position.

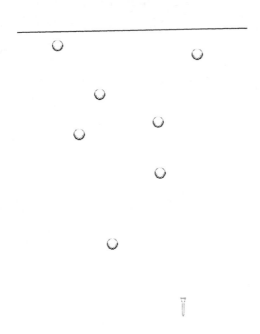

Putting games with your friends

Pac-man

We all remember the great arcade game that is Pac-man & now you can play it at the golf course.

You are going to place 8 tees around a hole between 3 & 8 feet (whatever distance you choose) and then position yourselves at opposite tees on the circle.

If you hole your putt you move to the next tee, however if you miss your putt you have to stay where you are.

The first person to be caught by the other has been eaten and eliminated.

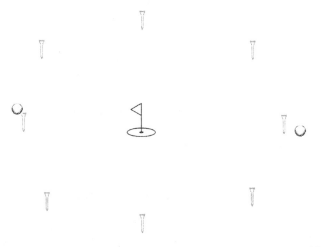

Stations

Now growing up I have heard many different names for this game like putting tennis, or putting ping pong, but my sister and I always called it stations.

This again is a great game to play with your friend and add in that little bit of friendly competition.

What you are going to do is set yourself at two different holes on the putting green that are anywhere between 8 -15 feet apart.

You are going to use one ball and take it in turns to try to hole the ball in the hole your friend is standing at. If you hole the putt, then you both have to switch places. The first person to reach 10 is the winner!

Chipping & Pitching Drills

Par 18

This is a great game to work on sharpening up your shortgame and boosting your up & downs out on the course.

What you are going to do is pick 9 different spots to hit from around the green. These are going to consist of 3 easy, 3 medium and 3 difficult locations. Now each of these mini holes is going to be a par 2 (we should make a chip & a putt), and by playing all 9 holes the total is "Par 18".

So, the aim of the game is to play all 9 holes and keep your score, with 18 being your target.

For example:

Hole 1 – 10yd chip   Hole 2 – downhill chip

Hole 3 – 30yd pitch   Hole 4 – 5yd chip

Hole 5 – bunker shot   Hole 6 – long rough pitch

Hole 7 – 15yd chip   Hole 8 – 20yd pitch

Hole 9 – uphill pitch

Umbrella / bucket challenge

When we are playing pitch shots out on the course our "landing zone" is extremely important (this is the part where the ball lands opposed to where it finishes) – This drill with the umbrella/bucket is a great way to work on those landing zones.

For this drill you will need a bucket or umbrella which you are going to place at various distances and see how many you can land in it out of 50 balls (10 each distance)

20 yards............................ /10

30yrds............................... /10

40yards.............................. /10

50yards.............................. /10

60 yards............................. /10

Driving range drills & games

Fairway Finder

Most driving ranges will have different distance markers or flags out on the range itself. These can be great for target practice and for "creating a fairway". What I want you to do is pick 2 targets that have about a 50-yard distance between them and then hit 10 balls. You're going to see how many balls out of those 10 you can get "in the fairway". This is a great drill that will help you visualise and simulate playing on the course 😊

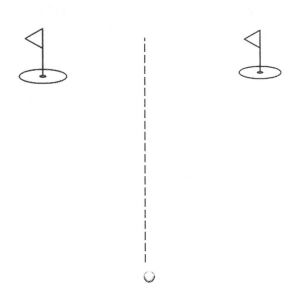

Play a hole

This is a great way to prepare yourself for getting out on the course as we all know that it is so different golfing on the range, to when we get out on the course.

With this drill I want you to imagine that you are playing a hole.

So, rather than just hitting 7 iron after 7 iron, I want you to pick a hole in your head, and play it how you would on the course. For example, your first shot with your driver, your second shot with your 6 iron, and then maybe a pitch. On the course we never get a second chance at playing a shot, and we have to go from woods to irons in a flash, so this drill helps you to practice that transition, and become more confident with it.

Chapter 13

Stories from other ladies

So, like I said earlier we are all in the same boat, and we all have highs & lows when it comes to this irritating yet beautifully addicting game! I thought it would be a good idea to bring you some stories from other ladies on their golf journey to give you all a giggle, get you motivated or to make you realise that we ALL go through the same things & feelings.

These are all true events, but I won't reveal any names! Enjoy...

*

"I had been playing for about 5 years and was asked to play for the Junior girls county team and because my handicap was the lowest, I was always sent out in the first match. I want to say that in 90% of those matches I ended up topping my first tee shot only 10 yards off the tee! (I always then went on to win my match of course)."

*

"One day I was playing golf with my husband and another couple when I was told by the other husband that I was only allowed to have 2 putts every hole, and I then had to pick up my ball, so I didn't "take too long". Funny part is he was allowed to three putt his way around the entire golf course!?"

*

"Let me tell you about one of my favourite golf memories. I was playing the last hole of a golf course where the green is right in front of the clubhouse bar. I've always struggled with the nerves of people watching but I hit an 8 iron that flew over the bunker and landed about 2 feet away from the pin. The whole terrace outside gave me huge cheer & applause, and as embarrassed as I was, it also felt amazing."

*

"I was once playing a tournament and wasn't aware that you are able to take a penalty shot and declare a ball "unplayable" if you cannot get it out of a bunker (a 2 shot penalty to drop out). It took me 22 shots to get out and I made a 28 on the hole. Whoops."

*'

"I was playing a Strokeplay tournament when I was about 10, but I knew it was not my day from the first hole. My grandparents caught up with me after 9 holes and asked how I was getting on. To this day they still laugh at my response which was "Oh I don't know, I picked my ball up already".."

*

"One of my funniest ever stories has to be from when I was playing in the British amateur in Ireland. Being a links course and right by the sea, the weather was brutal, and the wind was howling. My playing partner, who happened to be my friend, was dying for the toilet but there wasn't one to be seen. Us golf girls have all been brought up to just find a bush and go to the toilet, but the weather that day didn't make it an easy experience. My friend shouted from behind the bush that she needed her waterproof trousers asap... It turned out that going to the toilet whilst facing a gale force wind was not an ideal situation and basically, she had soaked herself in the process. Honestly that was about 15 years ago and it still makes me chuckle to this day."

*

"Let me tell you about my HOLE IN ONE! I can remember it still like it was yesterday and honestly, I think it will always be one of the best days of my golfing life. I was playing at Wentworth which is a very well-known golf course, and I was absolutely terrified to be there. Before I started, I had no idea how I was going to get around such a challenging course, yet here I was making a hole in one. Amazing!"

*

"Golf has given me so much extra confidence in everything I do. I honestly think that playing the game has helped me as a person in life to have a little more belief in myself."

*

"Last year I won my first ever trophy. It was a ladies stableford competition, and honestly after 15 years of golfing I never thought it would be a possibility. I have persevered over the years, and sometimes felt like giving up, but winning that competition made me realise you can do anything if you persevere and stay patient."

*

"I think one of the most embarrassing yet hilarious things that has ever happened to me was when I was at the range once. I don't even know how I managed it, but I was working really hard on "swinging through the ball", and somehow ended up doing a massive spin after hitting the ball and ended up on my bum. Honestly, I was mortified, but also in absolute hysterics. I think the shot was actually a good one to!!"

*

"I want to tell you about my best memory in golf. It was a few years ago now, but I can still remember it like it was yesterday. It was my first ever time on the golf course and I was playing with a lady who had been playing for a few years. I don't know how it happened but somehow on the 8th hole I hit my 3rd shot that scuttled up to the green and went in the hole, on a par 4! My first time on the course and I had made a birdie! Honestly you couldn't bring my head down from the clouds, I was ecstatic."

*

" The first time I played with my dad and his friends (who are all men at my club) I could tell that they weren't too keen on having me play with them and obviously expected me to play off the forward/red tees so were very surprised when I stepped up to tee off the yellows with them. On the second hole (as our first is a par 3) I outdrove them all from the same tees and proceeded to beat them all and take the money at the end of the round. Compliment of the day was "not bad, for a girl" and they obviously enjoyed my company as playing with them is now pretty much a weekly occurrence."

*

"Have you ever heard of someone hitting themselves with a golf ball before!? Well now you have... Don't ask me how I managed it, because I really do not know the answer to that. All I know is that I attempted to hit the ball and somehow the ball instead hit me in the leg haha! I dusted myself off though and carried on (with a slight limp haha)."

"Getting to play golf every week with some great friends really is what makes life fun. It doesn't matter whether we've played good or bad, we still have the best time every time."

"I was playing a par 5 and decided that today was the day I was going to go for the green with my 3rd shot rather than laying up in front of the water like I normally do. I took out my hybrid, took a deep breath, and went for it. My ball, in what felt like slow motion, sailed through the air, and landed about 2 feet over the water. When I tell you my heart nearly came out of my throat, I am not exaggerating haha, but I have also never felt more confident."

Chapter 14

Your Golfing Goals

Your 1-month goals

Your 6-month goals

Your 1-year goals

Your 5-year goals

Chapter 15

The MANuscript

How you can help the lady golfer in your life.

- Number 1 – ENCOURAGE! You should only ever show your partner support and encouragement along her journey.
- If she plays a bad shot do not sigh or ask, "why did you do that", simply let her know it's only one shot and onto the next.
- No unsolicited advice. Only offer your opinions & guidance if you have been asked for help.
- Offer your partner to come and play with you. The more a person can get out onto the course and play, the more their confidence is built. Being able to go out with you will feel more comforting than random people, so make the time on a weekend afternoon.
- Let her know you make mistakes too. If you talk about the bad shots and bad rounds of your own, you are making this feel normal. Ladies get so nervous about "playing bad". The more they know you do it too, the better they will feel about their own golf.

- Reinforce pride in the fact that they are playing a sport, and not only a sport, but one that is so challenging.
- Make sure that it remains an enjoyable activity rather than a forced obligation. The more you push, the more you are liable to push your partner from wanting to play. At the end of the day, it's just a bit of fun.
- Remember sportsmanship like you would with anyone. No one likes to be gloated at excessively ha.
- Be patient.
- Don't be too overly generous with giving putts. You may think this is saving your female playing partner from having to make a putt, but instead it takes away the satisfaction of holing the putt and finishing the hole.
- Women are not slow golfers, so please don't ever make a woman rush just because that is what people believe.
- Refrain from using the following terms about your own game, when playing with a lady "I got it caught in my skirt" or "oh I dropped my lipstick with that putt". These sayings aren't cute, and they aren't funny. Playing a bad shot and referring to yourself as a girl isn't what we want to hear.
- My final point is to enjoy the fact that you have a wife, partner, family member or friend who

136

wants to play golf. You are so lucky that they do, so just go and have fun together out on the course.

Golf is never perfect, and more than likely neither is the first edition of this book, but I have loved the journey of both with all my heart.

I really hope you have enjoyed reading the book and have been able to take away a few things to help you on your golfing journey.

I just want to finish by saying that I would like to dedicate this book to everyone who have helped me throughout my life with my golf (You all know who you are). I have been unbelievably lucky to have received the best support and love from family & friends.

Here is to making golf a women's world!!

Lots of Love, Abbey X

I would love to hear your stories and connect with you all further, so please reach out on my social media channels- @AbbeyGittingsGolf (Facebook, Instagram)

Or head over to the "Little Pink Girls Golf Lounge" on my website:
www.abbeygittingsgolfcoaching.com

Made in United States
North Haven, CT
09 April 2023